Solo Express

for the Beginning Percussionist

James Campbell

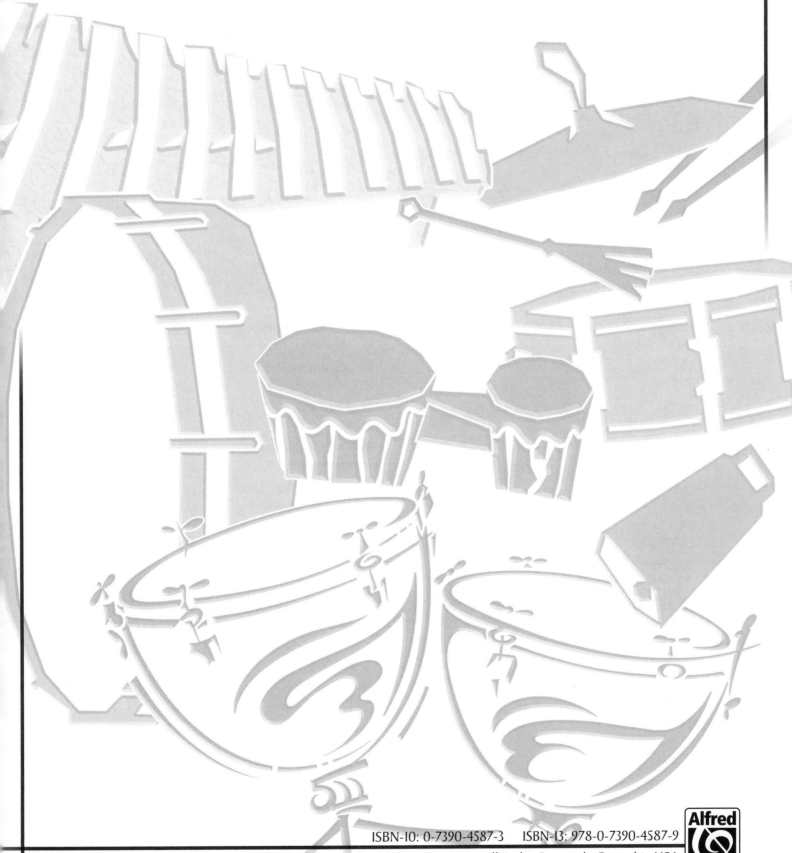

ISBN-10: 0-7390-4587-3   ISBN-13: 978-0-7390-4587-9

©2007 Alfred Publishing Co., Inc. • All Rights Reserved • Printed in USA

Alfred

Table of Contents

Solos

About the Author

James Campbell has received worldwide recognition as a performer, teacher, composer, author, and is a respected figure in the development of the contemporary percussion ensemble. He has toured extensively throughout North and Central America, Europe, and Asia. Currently, he is Professor of Music and Director of Percussion Studies at the University of Kentucky in Lexington, and also holds the positions of principal percussionist with the Lexington Philharmonic, drummer with the Kentucky Jazz Repertory Orchestra, and past-president of the Percussive Arts Society (PAS).

Well known for his long past association with the internationally renowned Rosemont Cavaliers Drum and Bugle Corps, Jim has served as their principal instructor, arranger, and program coordinator. He was percussion director for the McDonald's All-American High School Band, and has performed at the International Society of Music Education World Conference, Journèes de la Percussion, MENC National In-Service Conference, Midwest Band & Orchestra Clinic, MusicFest Canada, All-Japan Band Clinic, Texas Bandmasters Association, Bands of America World Percussion Symposium, and at several Percussive Arts Society International Conventions.

His numerous works for concert and marching percussion are published with Hal Leonard Publishing, C.L. Barnhouse Co., C. Alan Publications, Innovative Percussion, Row-Loff Productions, HoneyRock Publishing, Meredith Music and Alfred Publishing Co., with whom he serves as percussion team author for the *Expressions*™ Music Curriculum. He won First Place in the PAS 2005 Composition Contest for his work, *Garage Drummer*, scored for multiple-percussion solo with CD accompaniment.

Jim is an endorsee for Innovative Percussion, Evans Drumheads, and is a member of the Latin Percussion Educational Advisory Board. He is a clinician for the Avedis Zildjian Cymbal Company and a Performing Artist for the Yamaha Corporation of America, Band & Orchestral Instruments Division.

Preface

Solo Expressions for the Beginning Percussionist is designed as a sequential introduction of skills, techniques, and knowledge through the performance of 40 solos for the percussionist. The solos are designed to take the percussionist from the first experiences of a novice to that of a developing musician through the sequential development of individual and ensemble skills. Although the ordering of solos is designed to provide the student with sequential experiences in total percussion, it is also possible to play all of the solos in only one of the areas before experiencing other areas. Each solo is accompanied by a play-along CD track that coordinates with the individual solo and contains a short introduction that lets the percussionist experience the meter, volume, tempo, and style before they begin to play.

Percussion Instruments

Snare drum music may be performed on any suitable membrane instrument, including a practice pad. Students should adjust the level of the playback volume to balance with the play-along CD track accompaniment.

It is encouraged that students play the keyboard percussion solos on a variety of instruments, such as the standard bell kit, glockenspiel, xylophone, vibraphone, and marimba.

If timpani are not available, any two membrane instruments (high and low) may be substituted. Concert toms, bongos, timbales, or drumset toms are suggested alternatives; these will give the student percussionist experience with changing tones.

Student Equipment

The advancing percussion student must be required to provide the proper implements and accessories to participate fully in the comprehensive instrumental music program. A wide variety of mallets and instruments are necessary to properly study and perform percussion music. A stick bag or case will help protect equipment and accessories from damage. A black hand-sized towel should be placed on a flat music stand or table to help accommodate silent mallet changes.

Drum Rudiments

Drum rudiments, often thought of as the "scales" of drum technique, are fundamental sticking and rhythm patterns that are used in percussion playing. To develop one's technique, it is essential to practice drum rudiments. The 40 Percussive Arts Society (PAS) International Drum Rudiments consist of the 26 traditional rudiments alongside a number of orchestral, European, and contemporary hybrid rudiments.

Rudiments should be practiced with a "slow-fast-slow" (also referred to as "open-closed-open") approach. Start each rudiment slowly, and gradually increase the speed until the student reaches the fastest tempo that they can control. They should maintain that top speed and then gradually decrease the speed returning to their original starting tempo. The entire time limit of this approach should last from 60-120 seconds for each rudiment "breakdown." The overall time limit can naturally increase with experience and stamina. Strive to maintain a consistent overall volume and characteristic tone quality throughout each rudiment breakdown.

Solo Expressions for the Beginning Percussionist introduces ten of these rudiments in a progressive level of difficulty that is musically appropriate and pedagogically sound, and sequences their learning to fulfill music curriculum expectations:

1. Single-Stroke Roll – alternating strokes.
2. Multiple-Bounce Roll – creating multiple rebounds from a single stroke.
3. Single Paradiddle – single and double stroke combinations.
4. Flam – performing changing stick heights to create a grace note.
5. 5-Stroke Roll – termination of rebound strokes.
6. 9-Stroke Roll – extended time value of rebound strokes.
7. Flam tap – combining two rudiments.
8. Drag – changing stick heights to create lengthened grace notes.
9. Double-Stroke Roll – controlled rebound strokes.
10. 17-Stroke Roll – extended time value of controlled rebound strokes.

Roll and Drag Interpretation

The style of music and the characteristic response of the specific percussion instrument will determine whether to play a single-stroke roll, multiple-bounce roll or a double-stroke roll to sustain the sound. A single-stroke roll sounds best on resonant percussion instruments such as timpani, bass drum, marimba, xylophone, and suspended cymbal.

On the snare drum, all measured rolls and drags can be interpreted with either multiple-bounce strokes or double strokes. Although most concert music sounds best with closed rolls, students should continually practice both styles to develop their technique. Multiple-bounce rolls (closed style) are used to create a smooth and connected sound in concert band and orchestral music. Double-stroke rolls (open style) produce an articulate and controlled sound, and can be used when the music is majestic in nature, as in a march or when the roll needs to be an articulate voice. Ultimately, let the musical style dictate the choice of roll interpretation. Although the dynamic level and tempo of the music will ultimately determine the correct roll base (stroke speed), it is helpful for young students to use the sixteenth note as the roll base for duple meters.

Guidelines for Music in *Solo Expressions for the Beginning Percussionist*

Each solo is accompanied by two tracks: 1) a complete track containing the pre-recorded solo and 2) a play-along track to practice and perform with. Listen to the complete track, which includes the play-along accompaniment with the recorded solo instrument, before practicing with the track that only contains the play-along music. By listening first, the student will get an idea of the style of the music and hear a model recording of the characteristic sound quality of the instrument at the proper performance tempo.

Practice the solo (without the recording) by using a metronome set at a slower tempo. Once the student has control of their implements and is happy with their quality of sound, they can practice with the play-along track and then perform for family and friends.

Acknowledgments

I wish to thank Steve Houghton (project editor), Robert Parks, Andy Salmon, Ray Ulibari, Julie Hill, Julie Davila, Amy Smith, Andy Bliss, Ralph Hicks, Brian Perez, Colin Campbell and Nancy Campbell for their assistance.

SOLO 1

The Woodpecker

James Campbell

Snare Drum
- New material: Quarter notes and rests
- Play with full, relaxed strokes and avoid tension.
- The proper playing area on the drum is slightly off-center with the stick tips close together.
- Change in playing area (= play on rim)
- Maintain a smooth tone and an even volume level as you switch hands.

Count off:

SOLO 2

Rockin' on F

James Campbell

Keyboard Percussion

- New material: Fermata (hold note at least twice as long as marked)
- Play with full, relaxed strokes and avoid tension.
- Play in the center of the tone bar. When two mallets play the same bar, they should "split" the center.
- The best tone is achieved when the mallet is immediately lifted off the tone bar.
- Adjust the music stand height so the bottom of the stand is at keyboard height and as close to the instrument as possible.

Count off:

SOLO 3

Country Lane

James Campbell

Snare Drum
- New material: Eighth notes
- Play with full, relaxed strokes and avoid tension.
- The proper playing area on the drum is slightly off-center with the stick tips close together.
- Maintain a smooth tone and an even volume level as you switch hands.

Count off:

Tempo ♩ = 102

SOLO 4

Lift-Off

James Campbell

Timpani (Tune F-F)

- New material: Half notes and whole notes
- Substitute any pair of membrane instruments (high and low) if necessary.
- Play with full, relaxed strokes and avoid tension.
- The best playing area is 4"–5" from the edge of the bowl, directly over the pedal.
- The best tone is achieved when the mallet naturally rebounds off the head.
- Maintain a smooth tone and an even volume level as you switch hands.

Count off:

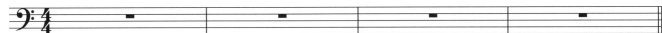

Tempo ♩ = 112

5   Let all notes ring.

9

13

17

21

25

SOLO 5

Flat Tire

James Campbell

Keyboard Percussion
- New material: Notes: E♭ and D
- Play with full, relaxed strokes and avoid tension.
- The suggested sticking helps to avoid wide leaps by one hand.
- Keep your eyes on the music, and use peripheral vision to locate the tone bars.
- Avoid raising the forearms or turning the wrist in order to reach the tone bars.

Count off:

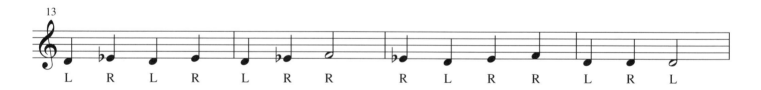

SOLO 6

Hot and Cold

James Campbell

Multiple Percussion: 2 Snare Drums (High = Snares On/Low = Snares Off)
- New material: Changing volume levels (dynamics)
- Place the high drum on the player's right and the low drum on the player's left.
- Substitute any pair of membrane instruments (high and low) if necessary.
- The proper playing area on the drum is slightly off-center with the stick tips close together.
- Maintain a smooth tone and an even volume level as you switch drums.

11 **1** 12

Count off:

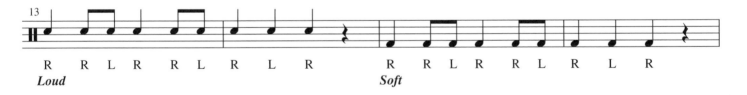

SOLO 7

Bounce Beat

James Campbell

Snare Drum

- New material: Multiple-bounce stroke (**Z** = let stick bounce many times on the drumhead)
- Keep the sticks lower to the head when first learning the multiple-bounce stroke in order to allow the sticks to bounce easier.
- Experiment with the amount of finger pressure needed to yield the most number of bounces for each multiple-bounce stroke.

Count off:

Tempo ♩ = 120

SOLO 8

Climbing Wall

James Campbell

Timpani (Tune B♭-F)

- New material: Key of B♭
- Substitute any pair of membrane instruments (high and low) if necessary.
- Listen carefully to your instrument and strive for the best sound quality at all times.
- The best playing area is 4"–5" from the edge of the bowl, directly over the pedal.
- The best tone is achieved when the mallet naturally rebounds off the head.

15 **1** 16

Count off:

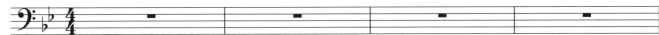

SOLO 9

Ambos a Dos
(From Me to You)

Puerto Rican Folk Song
Arr. James Campbell

17 **1** 18

Keyboard Percussion
- New material: Key of B♭; Notes: B♭ and C
- Play with full, relaxed strokes and avoid tension.
- Stand away from the keyboard, at a distance that puts the head of the mallets over the center of the lower row of tone bars.
- Keep your eyes on the music, and use peripheral vision to locate the tone bars.
- Avoid raising the forearms or turning the wrist in order to reach the tone bars.

Count off:

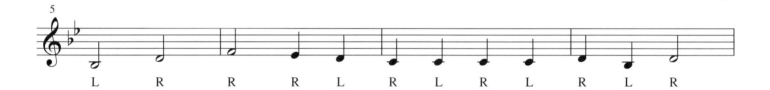

SOLO 10

Gemini

James Campbell

Bongos

- Review: Multiple drums (untuned)
- Substitute any pair of membrane instruments (high and low) if necessary.
- The drums should be flat and parallel to the floor. Adjust the stand so that the top heads are approximately waist-level or slightly below.
- Use snare-drum sticks or multi-percussion mallets.
- Play with full, relaxed strokes and avoid tension.

Count off: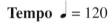

Tempo ♩ = 120

SOLO II

Stress Out

James Campbell

Snare Drum

- New material: Accents (more emphasis), dynamic markings (volume)
- Review: Multiple-bounce strokes (**z** = bounce stroke)
- When playing an accent, the stroke technique does not change. Vary the height of the implement to create the emphasis.
- Play with full, relaxed strokes and avoid tension.

Count off:

SOLO 12

Island Jam

James Campbell

Keyboard Percussion

- New material: Tied notes
- Review: Dynamic markings
- Use alternate sticking (R-L-R-L) where possible.
- Use consecutive sticking (R-R, L-L) to avoid crossing the mallets.
- Keep your eyes on the music, and use peripheral vision to locate the tone bars.

Count off:

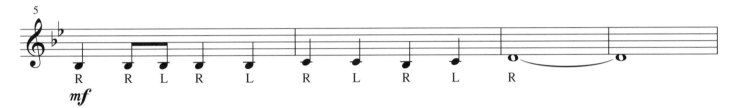

SOLO 13

A Little Diddle

James Campbell

Snare Drum
- New material: Single paradiddles (sticking = R-L-R-R or L-R-L-L)
- Maintain an even volume and stroke height on the consecutive stickings (diddles) when performing a paradiddle.
- Maintain contact on the stick with all fingers.
- Change in playing area (x = strike sticks together above the drum)

25 1 26

Count off:

SOLO 14

The Storm

James Campbell

27 **1** 28

Timpani (Tune B♭-F)

- New material: Single-stroke rolls
- Review: Changing dynamics
- Substitute any pair of membrane instruments (high and low) if necessary.
- Listen carefully to your instrument and strive for the best sound quality at all times.

Count off:

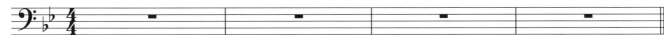

SOLO 15

Android

James Campbell

Keyboard Percussion
- New material: Notes: A♭ and G
- Use alternate sticking where possible.
- To make the music flow smoothly, it may be necessary to double stick on one hand.
  As a rule of thumb, double stick the notes that are nearer to each other rather than
  those that require a leap. Double stick accidental keys to naturals rather than naturals
  to accidentals; this will prevent awkward mallet movement.
- Keep your eyes on the music, and use peripheral vision to locate the tone bars.

29 **1** 30

Count off:

SOLO 16

Flam Jam

James Campbell

Snare Drum
- New material: Flams
- Review: Dynamic changes
- To perform a flam, one hand starts as the main note (high stroke position) and the other hand starts as the grace note (low stroke position). When both sticks are dropped simultaneously, the grace note strikes the head slightly ahead of the main note.

SOLO 17

Three by Three

James Campbell

Snare Drum
- New material: ¾ time signature
- Review: Multiple-bounce stroke, single paradiddles and flams
- Stay relaxed, avoid tension and always strive for good sound quality.

SOLO 18

Ghost Story

James Campbell

35 **1** 36

Keyboard Percussion

- New material: Key of E♭; Notes: Low and high A♭, low G, low and high A♮, high B♭
- Use alternate sticking where possible.
- To make the music flow smoothly, it may be necessary to double stick on one hand. As a rule of thumb, double stick the notes that are nearer to each other rather than those that require a leap. Double stick accidental keys to naturals rather than naturals to accidentals; this will prevent awkward mallet movement.
- Keep your eyes on the music, and use peripheral vision to locate the tone bars.

Count off:

SOLO 19

Tribal Dance

James Campbell

Timpani (Tune B♭-F)

- Substitute any pair of membrane instruments (high and low) if necessary.
- Maintain a relaxed grip and a smooth stroke motion while playing the single-stroke rolls.
- Use alternate sticking where possible.
- To make the music flow smoothly, it may be necessary to double stick on one hand. Double stick notes that are between the two drums, rather than those that are on the same drum.

SOLO 20

Sidecar

James Campbell

39 **1** 40

Multiple Percussion: Snare Drum (⬗) and Bongos (▽⼀▽)
- Review: Multiple-bounce stroke, flams and ¾ time signature
- Place the bongos across from the player, between the snare drum and the music stand.
- Substitute any pair of membrane instruments (high and low) if necessary.
- Maintain a smooth tone and an even volume level as you switch drums.

SOLO 21

Stop Time

James Campbell

Multiple Percussion: Snare Drum (◩) and Woodblock (▭)
- New material: Eighth-note rests, syncopation, and crescendos
- Place the woodblock on a padded surface or mount it on a stand.
- Experiment with playing areas to find the exact "sweet spot" (the area that yields the best tone) on the woodblock.

SOLO 22

Can-Can

Offenbach
Arr. James Campbell

Keyboard Percussion

- Use alternate sticking where possible.
- To make the music flow smoothly, it may be necessary to double stick on one hand. As a rule of thumb, double stick the notes that are nearer to each other rather than those that require a leap. Double stick accidental keys to naturals rather than naturals to accidentals; this will prevent awkward mallet movement.
- Keep your eyes on the music, and use peripheral vision to locate the tone bars.

Count off:

SOLO 23

Working 9 to 5

James Campbell

Snare Drum

- New material: Double-stroke roll, 5-stroke roll, and 9-stroke roll
- Review: Crescendos and decrescendos/diminuendos
- A double-stroke roll is similar to a multiple-bounce roll, but the stick bounces twice per stroke rather than multiple times.
- To create a double stroke, the grip pressure between the thumb and first finger should be less firm than what is needed to produce a multiple-bounce stroke, but controlled so that the double-bounce rhythm is clear.
- Strive to create an even and balanced sound between hands as you play double strokes.
- A 5-stroke roll = 2 multiple- or double-bounce strokes followed by an accented single stroke.
- A 9-stroke roll = 4 multiple- or double-bounce strokes followed by an accented single stroke.

SOLO 24

Jungle Jim

James Campbell

Timpani (Tune G-D)

- Review: Single-stroke roll, crescendos and decrescendos/diminuendos
- Substitute any pair of membrane instruments (high and low) if necessary.
- The best tone is achieved when the mallet naturally rebounds off the head.
- Let all tones ring (do not dampen or mute the head of the drum).

SOLO 25

Flam City

James Campbell

Snare Drum

- New material: $\frac{2}{4}$ time signature, flam taps and sixteenth-note rhythms
- When playing alternating flams, sticks should make a quick exchange between the grace note and the main note as they rebound from hand to hand.
- The "flam tap" rudiment starts with two notes of the same value in a row. The first note is played as a flam. The second note, or "tap," is played with the same hand that played the main note of the flam.

Count off:

Tempo ♩ = 98

SOLO 26

Dance of the Reed Flutes

Tchaikovsky
Arr. James Campbell

Keyboard Percussion

- New material: Note: Low A♮
- Maintain a relaxed grip and use a smooth, connected motion when playing a single-stroke roll. Strive for an even and balanced sound between hands.
- When playing on a xylophone or marimba, use a single-stroke roll to sustain longer note values.
- Use alternate sticking where possible.
- To make the music flow smoothly, it may be necessary to double stick on one hand. As a rule of thumb, double stick the notes that are nearer to each other rather than those that require a leap. Double stick accidental keys to naturals rather than naturals to accidentals; this will prevent awkward mallet movement.

Count off:

SOLO 27

Slip and Slide

James Campbell

Multiple Percussion: Snare Drum (◇) and Suspended Cymbal (—)

- New material: Technique: "Slide stroke" with brush (↭)
  Multiple implements: Stick (|) and brushes (⅄⅄)
- Place a black, hand-sized towel on a flat music stand or padded table to help facilitate silent and efficient implement changes.

Count off: ♩ ♩ ♩ | ♩ ♩ ♩

SOLO 28

Wild Horses

James Campbell

Timpani (Tune G-D)

- Substitute any pair of membrane instruments (high and low) if necessary.
- Avoid overplaying on the instrument when the rhythm becomes faster or more difficult.
- Use alternate sticking where possible.

SOLO 29

Cheki Morena

Puerto Rican Folk Song
Arr. James Campbell

17 **2** 18

Keyboard Percussion

- New material: Note: E; Key: F
- Maintain a relaxed grip and use a smooth, connected motion when playing a single-stroke roll. Strive for an even sound and dynamic level between hands.
- Use alternate sticking where possible.
- To make the music flow smoothly, it may be necessary to double stick on one hand. As a rule of thumb, double stick the notes that are nearer to each other rather than those that require a leap. Double stick accidental keys to naturals rather than naturals to accidentals; this will prevent awkward mallet movement.

SOLO 30

Rudiment Rumba

James Campbell

Multiple Percussion: Snare Drum (▱) and Cowbell (♩)

- Review: 5- and 9-stroke rolls, flams, flam taps and single paradiddles
- Place the cowbell on a padded surface or mount it on a stand.
- Experiment with playing areas to find the exact "sweet spot" (the area that yields the best tone) on the cowbell.
- Think of flams and drags as one downward motion that is made simultaneously by both sticks. Keep the grace note low and the main note high.

Count off: ♩ ♪ ♩ ♪ | ♩ ♩ ♩ ♩

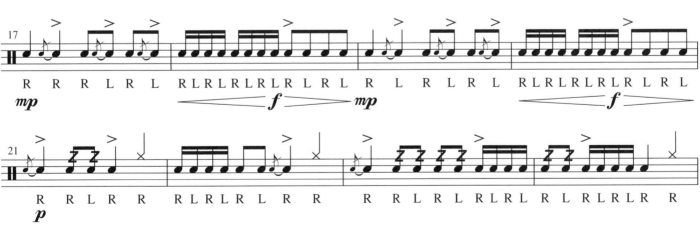

SOLO 31

Drag Race

James Campbell

Multiple Percussion: Snare Drum (◿), Woodblock (▱) and Cowbell (⌂)
- New material: Single drags
- The single-drag rudiment should be approached in the same way as a flam, with the "drag" taking the place of the lower grace note. The drag can be played either "open" (2 even bounces) or "closed" (multiple bounces).
- Place the hand instruments on a padded surface, or mount them on stands.
- Set up the woodblock (left side) and the cowbell (right side) on the opposite side of the snare drum from the player.

Count off:

SOLO 32

Double Trouble

James Campbell

Snare Drum

- New material: 17-stroke roll
- To create a double stroke, the grip pressure between the thumb and first finger should be less firm than what is needed to produce a multiple-bounce stroke, but controlled so that the double-bounce rhythm is clear.
- Strive to create an even and balanced sound between hands as you play double strokes.

Count off:

SOLO 33

Kite Festival

James Campbell

25 **2** 26

Keyboard Percussion

- New material: Note: High C
- Use alternate sticking where possible.
- To make the music flow smoothly, it may be necessary to double stick on one hand. As a rule of thumb, double stick the notes that are nearer to each other rather than those that require a leap. Double stick accidental keys to naturals rather than naturals to accidentals; this will prevent awkward mallet movement.

Count off:

SOLO 34

Rush Hour

James Campbell

27 **2** 28

Timpani (Tune B♭-F)

- Substitute any pair of membrane instruments (high and low) if necessary.
- Let all tones ring (do not dampen or mute the head of the drum).
- Listen carefully to your instrument and strive for the best sound quality at all times.
- Use alternate sticking where possible.
- To make the music flow smoothly, it may be necessary to double stick on one hand. Double stick notes that are between the two drums, rather than those that are on the same drum.

Count off:

Tempo ♩ = 116

SOLO 35

America
(My Country, 'Tis of Thee)

Traditional
Arr. James Campbell

Keyboard Percussion
- New material: Legato stroke
- To create a legato start to each note, keep a relaxed grip and use a very fluid, full stroke. Let the mallet rebound naturally, and allow the instrument's sound to decay on its own, without dampening.
- When playing on a xylophone or marimba, use a single-stroke roll to sustain longer note values.

Count off:

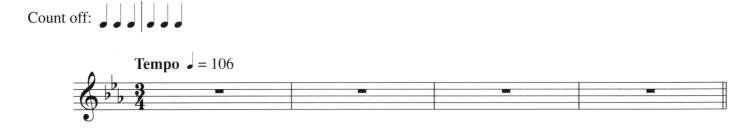

SOLO 36

Along for the Ride

James Campbell

Multiple Percussion: Snare Drum (◺) and Suspended Cymbal (♩)

- New material: "Slash" notation for rolls
- Set up the cymbal (right side) on the opposite side of the snare drum from the player. The right hand plays all cymbal notes.
- Use sixteenth notes as a roll base, and play in either an open (double-bounce) or closed (multiple-bounce) style.

Count off: ♩ 𝄾 ♩ 𝄾 | ♩ ♩ ♩ ♩

SOLO 37

Step on the Gas

James Campbell

Multiple Percussion: Snare Drum (◺) and Kick Bass Drum (◻)
- Set up the bass drum so that the foot pedal can be comfortably reached.
- Use a stool or a drum throne if desired.
- Keep the entire foot relaxed and in contact with the pedal throughout the stroke ("kick").

33 **2** 34

Count off:

Tempo ♩ = 120

SOLO 38

Surf's Up

James Campbell

Snare Drum

- Review: The 10 fundamental drum rudiments.
- Use sixteenth notes as a roll base, and play in either an open (double-bounce) or closed (multiple-bounce) style.
- Think of flams and drags as one downward motion that is made simultaneously by both sticks. Keep the grace note low and the main note high.

SOLO 39

Eine Kleine Nachtmusik

Mozart
Arr. James Campbell

37 **2** 38

Keyboard Percussion

- New material: Dotted-note rhythms, staccato (·) articulation
- To create a staccato start to marked notes, use a very quick stroke. Lift the mallet quickly off the bar to give a more marked feel.
- Listen carefully to the sound of your instrument and always strive for the proper tone quality and dynamic level.